JELL-O® **CoolWhip**® **Baker's**®

Holiday Desserts

Publications International Ltd.

Favorite Brand Name Recipes at www.fbnr.com

Microwave Cooking: Microwave ovens vary in wattage. Use the cooking times as guidelines and check for doneness before adding more time.

Preparation/Cooking Times: Preparation times are based on the approximate amount of time required to assemble the recipe before cooking, baking, chilling, or serving. These times include preparation steps such as measuring, chopping, and mixing. The fact that some preparations and cooking can be done simultaneously is taken into account. Preparation of optional ingredients and serving suggestions is not included.

contents

29

58

9

81

WHIPPED TOPPING

SINCE 1780

The holiday season is the time of year we dedicate to creating lasting memories with family and friends. Festivities abound during this busy season, and food is often at the center. From gift exchanges to open houses to that special holiday meal, sweet treats and show stopper desserts are a must have.

The dessert table is where holiday memories are created. A new holiday favorite can turn into an instant classic to be shared and enjoyed for years to come.

We've dedicated this collection of recipes to helping you create new holiday favorites for your family. To help you find the perfect recipe for your next holiday gathering, we've divided this book into five sections:

- **Chocolate Sensations:** A collection of rich, irresistible chocolaty desserts.

- **Fresh-Baked Gift Exchange:** Dessert ideas that make perfect gifts.

- **Fast & Fabulous Entertaining:** Stress-free desserts that are sure to wow all your guests.

- **Delicious Desserts for Kids:** Fun recipes children will love to make and eat.

- **Holiday Classics:** Timeless favorites and new dessert creations.

We hope you enjoy this great collection of holiday desserts that are sure to dazzle your family and friends. From all of us at the Kraft Kitchens, we hope this holiday season is the sweetest ever...

chocolate
sensations

A collection of rich, irresistible chocolaty desserts
featuring everyone's favorite flavor of the season

MOLTEN CHOCOLATE CAKES

Total: 29 minutes

4 squares **BAKER'S** Semi-Sweet Baking Chocolate

½ cup (1 stick) butter

1 cup powdered sugar

2 eggs

2 egg yolks

6 tablespoons flour

Additional powdered sugar and fresh raspberries (optional)

PREHEAT oven to 425°F. Butter 4 (¾-cup) custard cups or soufflé dishes. Place on baking sheet.

MICROWAVE chocolate and butter in large microwaveable bowl on HIGH 1 minute or until butter is melted. Stir with wire whisk until chocolate is completely melted. Stir in 1 cup powdered sugar until well blended. Blend in eggs and egg yolks with wire whisk. Stir in flour. Divide batter between prepared custard cups.

BAKE 13 to 14 minutes or until sides are firm but centers are soft. Let stand 1 minute. Carefully run small knife around cakes to loosen. Invert cakes onto dessert dishes. Serve immediately each topped with additional powdered sugar and garnish with raspberries, if desired.

Makes 8 servings, ½ molten cake each.

MAKE AHEAD: Batter can be made a day ahead. Pour into prepared custard cups. Cover with plastic wrap. Refrigerate. Bake as directed.

JAZZ IT UP: Top each serving with a small dollop of thawed **COOL WHIP** Whipped Topping.

CHOCOLATE PASSION BOWL

Total: 1 hour 20 minutes (includes refrigerating)

3 cups cold milk

2 packages (4-serving size each) **JELL-O** Chocolate Flavor Instant
    Pudding & Pie Filling

1 tub (8 ounces) **COOL WHIP** French Vanilla Whipped Topping,
    thawed, divided

1 baked (9-inch-square) brownie layer, cooled, cut into 1-inch cubes
    (about 5½ cups)

1 pint (2 cups) raspberries

POUR milk into large bowl. Add dry pudding mixes. Beat with wire whisk
2 minutes or until well blended. Gently stir in 1 cup of the whipped
topping.

PLACE half of the brownie cubes in 2-quart serving bowl; top with half
each of the pudding mixture, raspberries and the remaining whipped
topping. Repeat all layers.

REFRIGERATE at least 1 hour or until ready to serve. Store leftover
dessert in refrigerator.

Makes 16 servings, about ⅔ cup each.

JAZZ IT UP: Chop 2 chocolate-coated caramel-peanut nougat bars
(2.07 ounces each). Assemble dessert as directed, topping each
layer of raspberries with layer of half of the chopped nougat bars.

chocolate sensations

EASY MIDNIGHT TRUFFLES

Total: 3 hours 20 minutes (includes refrigerating)

6 squares **BAKER'S** Semi-Sweet Baking Chocolate

2 squares **BAKER'S** Unsweetened Baking Chocolate

6 tablespoons butter or margarine

½ cup whipping cream

Suggested coatings: powdered sugar, finely chopped **PLANTERS** Walnuts, **BAKER'S ANGEL FLAKE** Coconut, unsweetened cocoa

MICROWAVE chocolates and butter in medium microwaveable bowl on HIGH 1½ minutes, stirring after 1 minute. Stir until well blended. Add whipping cream; mix well. Cover.

REFRIGERATE 3 hours or until firm.

SHAPE chocolate mixture into 36 balls, each about ½ inch in diameter. Roll in suggested coatings until evenly coated. Store in tightly covered container in refrigerator.

Makes 3 dozen or 12 servings, 3 truffles each.

MAKE-AHEAD: Mix chocolate mixture as directed; cover. Refrigerate up to 24 hours. Let stand at room temperature 1 hour to soften slightly before shaping into balls and rolling in suggested coatings as directed.

DOUBLE CHOCOLATE MOUSSE

Total: 30 minutes

1½ cups cold fat free milk, divided

2 squares **BAKER'S** Semi-Sweet Baking Chocolate

1 package (4-serving size) **JELL-O** Chocolate Flavor Fat Free Sugar Free Instant Reduced Calorie Pudding & Pie Filling

2 cups thawed **COOL WHIP FREE** Whipped Topping, divided

½ cup fresh raspberries

COMBINE 1 cup of the milk and the chocolate in large microwaveable bowl. Microwave on HIGH 2 minutes; stir until chocolate is completely melted. Stir in remaining ½ cup milk. Add dry pudding mix. Beat with wire whisk 2 minutes or until well blended. Refrigerate at least 20 minutes. Gently stir in 1½ cups of the whipped topping.

SPOON into 6 dessert dishes.

TOP with the remaining ½ cup whipped topping and the raspberries. Store leftover desserts in refrigerator.

Makes 6 servings, 1 dessert each.

MAKE AHEAD: Prepare as directed, except do not top with the remaining ½ cup whipped topping and the raspberries. Refrigerate until ready to serve. Top with the remaining whipped topping and the raspberries just before serving.

BAKER'S ONE BOWL Chocolate Fudge

10 Minute Prep

Total: 2 hours 10 minutes (includes refrigerating)

2 packages (8 squares each) **BAKER'S** Semi-Sweet Baking Chocolate

1 can (14 ounces) sweetened condensed milk

2 teaspoons vanilla

1 cup chopped **PLANTERS** Nuts or toasted **BAKER'S ANGEL FLAKE** Coconut (optional)

MICROWAVE chocolate and milk in large microwaveable bowl on HIGH 2 to 3 minutes or until chocolate is almost melted, stirring after each minute. Stir until chocolate is completely melted.

ADD vanilla and nuts; mix well. Spread into foil-lined 8-inch-square pan.

REFRIGERATE 2 hours or until firm. Cut into 1-inch squares.

Makes about 2 pounds or 16 servings,
3 (1-inch) squares per serving.

MAKE IT EASY: Lining pan with **REYNOLDS** foil makes cutting the fudge easier with little cleanup. Be sure to use enough foil to extend over the pan's edges—it becomes the handles for lifting the fudge out of the pan and onto a cutting board for easy cutting.

chocolate sensations

DECADENT TRIPLE LAYER MUD PIE

Total: 3 hours 25 minutes (includes refrigerating)

3 squares **BAKER'S** Semi-Sweet Baking Chocolate, melted

¼ cup canned sweetened condensed milk

1 **OREO** Pie Crust (6 ounces)

½ cup chopped **PLANTERS** Pecans, toasted

2 cups cold milk

2 packages (4-serving size each) **JELL-O** Chocolate Flavor Instant Pudding & Pie Filling

1 tub (8 ounces) **COOL WHIP** Whipped Topping, thawed, divided

MIX chocolate and condensed milk until well blended. Pour into crust; sprinkle with pecans.

POUR milk into large bowl. Add dry pudding mixes. Beat with wire whisk 2 minutes or until well blended. (Mixture will be thick.) Spoon 1½ cups of the pudding over pecans in crust. Add half of the whipped topping to remaining pudding; stir with wire whisk until well blended. Spread over pudding layer in crust; top with remaining whipped topping.

REFRIGERATE 3 hours. Store leftover pie in refrigerator.

Makes 10 servings, 1 slice each.

> **HOW TO TOAST NUTS:** Preheat oven to 350°F. Spread pecans in single layer in shallow baking pan. Bake 5 to 7 minutes or until lightly toasted, stirring occasionally.

OREO CHOCOLATE CREAM CHEESECAKE

Total: 2 hours 10 minutes (includes refrigerating)

32 **OREO** Chocolate Sandwich Cookies, divided

4 packages (8 ounces each) **PHILADELPHIA** Cream Cheese, softened

1 cup sugar

1 teaspoon vanilla

1 package (8 squares) **BAKER'S** Semi-Sweet Baking Chocolate, melted, slightly cooled

4 eggs

PREHEAT oven to 325°F if using a silver 9-inch springform pan (or to 300°F if using a dark nonstick 9-inch springform pan). Quarter 20 of the cookies; set aside. Finely crush remaining 12 cookies; press firmly onto bottom of greased pan. Bake 10 minutes.

BEAT cream cheese, sugar and vanilla with electric mixer on medium speed until well blended. Add chocolate; mix well. Add eggs, 1 at a time, mixing on low speed after each addition just until blended. Gently stir in 1½ cups of the quartered cookies. Pour over crust. Sprinkle with remaining quartered cookies.

BAKE 50 minutes to 1 hour or until center is almost set. Run knife or metal spatula around rim of pan to loosen cake; cool before removing rim of pan. Refrigerate 4 hours or overnight. Store leftover cheesecake in refrigerator.

Makes 16 servings, 1 slice each.

HOW TO TEST CHEESECAKE DONENESS: Check cheesecake doneness by gently shaking the pan. If the cheesecake is done, it will be set except for a small area in the center that will be soft and jiggly. Do not insert a knife into the center as this may cause the cheesecake to crack during cooling.

SUBSTITUTE: Prepare as directed, using **OREO** Chocolate Creme Chocolate Sandwich Cookies.

RASPBERRY GANACHE PIE

Total: 4 hours 15 minutes (includes refrigerating)

1 package (8 squares) **BAKER'S** Semi-Sweet Baking Chocolate,
  coarsely chopped

1 cup whipping cream

6 tablespoons seedless raspberry jam, divided

1 **OREO** Pie Crust (6 ounces)

2 cups raspberries

1 tablespoon water

PLACE chocolate in medium bowl; set aside. Mix cream and
2 tablespoons of the jam in small saucepan. Bring just to boil,
stirring constantly. Remove from heat. Pour over chocolate
in bowl. Let stand 2 minutes.

BEAT with wire whisk until chocolate is completely melted and
mixture is well blended. Pour into crust; cover. Refrigerate
4 hours or overnight.

ARRANGE raspberries on top of pie. Microwave remaining
¼ cup jam and water in small microwaveable bowl on HIGH
30 seconds; stir until well blended. Brush over raspberries.
Refrigerate until ready to serve.

Makes 10 servings, 1 slice each.

MAKE AHEAD: Pie can be prepared ahead of time. Cover and
freeze up to 2 days. Place in refrigerator to thaw about 2 hours
before serving.

DOUBLE CHOCOLATE NILLA SQUARES

Total: 3 hours 15 minutes (includes refrigerating)

- 64 **NILLA** Wafers, divided
- 3 tablespoons sugar
- 6 tablespoons butter or margarine, softened, divided
- 4 squares **BAKER'S** Semi-Sweet Baking Chocolate
- 2½ cups cold milk
- 2 packages (4-serving size each) **JELL-O** Chocolate Flavor Instant Pudding & Pie Filling
- 1½ cups (½ of 8-ounce tub) thawed **COOL WHIP** Whipped Topping

CRUSH 40 of the wafers; mix with sugar and 5 tablespoons of the butter until well blended. Press firmly onto bottom of 13×9-inch baking pan to form crust.

PLACE chocolate and remaining 1 tablespoon butter in small microwaveable bowl. Microwave on HIGH 1 minute or until butter is melted. Stir until chocolate is completely melted. Drizzle over crust with spoon.

POUR milk into large bowl. Add pudding mixes. Beat with wire whisk 2 minutes. Gently stir in whipped topping. Spread half of the pudding mixture over crust; top with remaining 24 wafers. Cover with remaining pudding mixture. Refrigerate at least 3 hours. Cut into 24 squares.

Makes 24 servings, 1 square each.

JAZZ IT UP: Garnish each square with an additional halved **NILLA** Wafer drizzled with chocolate.

chocolate sensations

BEST EVER CHOCOLATE FUDGE LAYER CAKE

Total: 1 hour 10 minutes

1 package (2-layer size) chocolate cake mix

1 package (4-serving size) **JELL-O** Chocolate Flavor Instant Pudding & Pie Filling

4 eggs

1 cup **BREAKSTONE'S** or **KNUDSEN** Sour Cream

½ cup vegetable oil

½ cup water

1 package (8 squares) **BAKER'S** Semi-Sweet Baking Chocolate, divided

1 tub (8 ounces) **COOL WHIP** Whipped Topping, thawed

2 tablespoons **PLANTERS** Sliced Almonds

PREHEAT oven to 350°F. Lightly grease 2 (9-inch) round cake pans. Beat cake mix, dry pudding mix, eggs, sour cream, oil and water in large bowl with electric mixer on low speed just until moistened, scraping side of bowl frequently. Beat on medium speed 2 minutes or until well blended. Stir in 2 squares of the chocolate, chopped. Spoon into prepared pans.

BAKE 30 to 35 minutes or until toothpick inserted near centers comes out clean. Cool in pans 10 minutes on wire rack. Loosen cakes from side of pans with spatula or knife. Invert cakes onto rack; gently remove pans. Cool completely on wire rack.

PLACE remaining 6 squares chocolate and whipped topping in medium microwaveable bowl. Microwave on HIGH 1½ to 2 minutes. Stir until well blended and shiny. Cool 5 minutes. Place 1 cake layer on serving plate; spread ¼ of the chocolate mixture over cake. Place second cake layer on top; spread remaining chocolate mixture over top and sides of cake. Garnish with almonds.

Makes 18 servings, 1 slice each.

fresh-baked gift exchange

Cookies, bars, and candy with a festive flair to give, trade, and share with loved ones

CHOCOLATE HOLIDAY BEARS

Total: 34 minutes

- ¾ cup (1½ sticks) butter or margarine, softened
- ¾ cup firmly packed brown sugar
- 1 package (4-serving size) **JELL-O** Chocolate Flavor Instant Pudding & Pie Filling
- 1 egg
- 1¾ cups flour
- 1 teaspoon baking soda
- 1 teaspoon ground cinnamon (optional)
- Decorations: assorted small candies, raisins, sprinkles, **JET-PUFFED** Miniature Marshmallows, colored sugars or licorice strips
- 3 squares **BAKER'S** Semi-Sweet Baking Chocolate

PREHEAT oven to 350°F. Beat butter, sugar, dry pudding mix and egg in large bowl with electric mixer on medium speed until well blended.

COMBINE remaining dry ingredients. Gradually add to pudding mixture, beating until well blended after each addition. Form into ball. (Refrigerate for up to 1 hour if dough is too soft to roll out.)

ROLL out dough on lightly floured surface to ¼-inch thickness. Cut out dough using 4-inch "bear" cookie cutter or other 4-inch holiday cookie cutter; place on greased baking sheets. Reroll scraps and use to cut additional cookies as needed.

BAKE 12 to 14 minutes or until slightly firm. Remove from baking sheets. Cool on wire racks. Decorate cutouts with small candies, raisins, sprinkles or marshmallows for eyes, mouth and buttons, pressing in lightly.

MELT chocolate in microwaveable bowl on MEDIUM (50%) for 2 minutes. Spread on bottom half of bears for pants or skirts; use as "glue" to attach more decorations.

Makes 20 servings, 1 cookie each.

SOFT & CHEWY CHOCOLATE DROPS

Total: 45 minutes (includes refrigerating)

4 squares **BAKER'S** Unsweetened Baking Chocolate

¾ cup (1½ sticks) butter

2 cups sugar

3 eggs

1 teaspoon vanilla

2 cups flour

PREHEAT oven to 350°F. Microwave chocolate and butter in large microwaveable bowl on HIGH 2 minutes or until butter is melted. Stir until chocolate is completely melted. Stir in sugar. Blend in eggs and vanilla. Add flour; mix well. Refrigerate 15 minutes or until dough is easy to handle.

SHAPE dough into 1-inch balls; place 2 inches apart on greased baking sheets.

BAKE 8 minutes or just until set. (Do not overbake.) Let stand on baking sheet 1 minute; transfer to wire racks. Cool completely.

Makes about 5 dozen or 30 servings,
2 cookies each.

MAKE AHEAD: To freeze, place balls of dough on wax paper-covered baking sheet; freeze until firm. Transfer to resealable freezer-weight plastic bag; freeze up to 3 months. Bake frozen balls 10 minutes or just until set.

VARIATION: For thicker Drops, increase flour to 2¼ cups.

SIMPLY SPECIAL CHOCOLATE BARK

Take 1 package (9 ounces) **BAKER'S** Dark Chocolate Melts and mix & match your recipe from these options...

Recipe options	topping choices
Caramel-Pecan Bark	½ cup **PLANTERS** Pecan Pieces; 10 **KRAFT** Caramels melted with 2 teaspoons water
Candy Cane Bark	¼ cup crushed peppermint candies (about 10 candies)
S'more Bark	½ cup **JET-PUFFED** Miniature Marshmallows; 2 **HONEY MAID** Honey Grahams, coarsely crushed (about ½ cup)
OREO Bark	7 **OREO** Chocolate Sandwich Cookies, coarsely chopped (about 1 cup)

Then follow our 3 simple steps:

1. **MICROWAVE** chocolate in medium microwaveable bowl on HIGH 2 minutes or until almost melted, stirring after 1 minute. Stir until chocolate is completely melted.

2. **SPREAD** half of the chocolate onto wax paper-covered baking sheet. Add **toppings**. Drizzle evenly with remaining chocolate.

3. **REFRIGERATE** 1½ hours or until firm. Break into 10 pieces. Store in tightly covered container in the refrigerator.

Makes 10 servings, 1 piece each.

HOW TO MELT CARAMELS: Place 10 **KRAFT** Caramels and 2 teaspoons water in small microwaveable bowl. Microwave on HIGH 30 seconds; stir until caramels are completely melted.

S'MORE BARK

JELL-O Pastel Cookies

Total: 40 minutes

3½ cups flour

1 teaspoon **CALUMET** Baking Powder

1½ cups (3 sticks) butter or margarine, softened

1 cup sugar

2 packages (4-serving size each) **JELL-O** Gelatin, any flavor, divided

1 egg

1 teaspoon vanilla

PREHEAT oven to 400°F. Mix flour and baking powder; set aside. Beat butter in large bowl with electric mixer on medium speed until creamy. Gradually add sugar and 1 package of the dry gelatin, beating until light and fluffy. Add egg and vanilla; mix well. Gradually add flour mixture, beating until well blended after each addition.

SHAPE dough into 1-inch balls. Place, 2 inches apart, on ungreased baking sheets. Flatten with bottom of clean glass. Sprinkle with remaining dry gelatin.

BAKE 8 to 10 minutes or until edges are lightly browned. Remove from baking sheets to wire racks. Cool completely. Store in tightly covered container at room temperature.

Makes about 5 dozen cookies or 30 servings, 2 cookies each.

MAKE AHEAD: To freeze, place balls of uncooked dough on wax paper-covered baking sheet; freeze until firm. Transfer to resealable freezer-weight plastic bag; freeze up to 3 months. Thaw on baking sheets before baking.

CRUNCH BARS

Total: 32 minutes

  35 **PREMIUM** Saltine Crackers

  ½ cup (1 stick) butter or margarine

  ½ cup firmly packed brown sugar

   1 package (8 squares) **BAKER'S** Semi-Sweet Baking Chocolate, chopped

   1 cup chopped **PLANTERS** Walnuts

PREHEAT oven to 400°F. Place crackers in **REYNOLDS** foil-lined 15×10×1-inch baking pan.

PLACE butter and sugar in saucepan; cook on medium-high heat until butter is completely melted and mixture is well blended, stirring occasionally. Bring to boil; boil 3 minutes without stirring. Spread over crackers.

BAKE 5 to 7 minutes or until topping is golden brown. Immediately sprinkle with chopped chocolate; let stand 5 minutes or until chocolate is softened. Spread chocolate evenly over ingredients in pan; sprinkle with walnuts. Cool. Break into pieces.

Makes 16 servings.

SHORTCUT: Use a food processor to quickly chop the walnuts.

BAKER'S ONE BOWL Coconut Macaroons

Total: 50 minutes

1 package (14 ounces) **BAKER'S ANGEL FLAKE** Coconut (5⅓ cups)

⅔ cup sugar

6 tablespoons flour

¼ teaspoon salt

4 egg whites

1 teaspoon almond extract

PREHEAT oven to 325°F. Grease and flour baking sheets; set aside. Mix coconut, sugar, flour and salt in large bowl. Stir in egg whites and almond extract until well blended.

DROP coconut mixture into 36 mounds, 2 inches apart, on prepared baking sheets, using about 1 tablespoonful of the coconut mixture for each mound.

BAKE 20 minutes or until edges are golden brown. Immediately remove from baking sheets to wire racks. Cool completely.

Makes 3 dozen or 18 servings, 2 cookies each.

CHOCOLATE-DIPPED MACAROONS: Prepare Coconut Macaroons as directed. Cool. Melt 1 package (8 squares) **BAKER'S** Semi-Sweet Baking Chocolate as directed on package. Dip cookies halfway into chocolate; let excess chocolate drip off. Let stand at room temperature or refrigerate on wax paper-lined tray 30 minutes or until chocolate is firm.

NO-OVEN PEANUT BUTTER SQUARES

Total: 1 hour 10 minutes (includes refrigerating)

½ cup (1 stick) butter or margarine

2 cups powdered sugar

1½ cups **NABISCO** Graham Cracker Crumbs

1 cup peanut butter

1½ packages (12 squares) **BAKER'S** Semi-Sweet Baking Chocolate

LINE 13×9-inch baking pan with **REYNOLDS** foil, with ends of foil extending over sides of pan. Set aside.

MELT butter in large microwaveable bowl on HIGH 45 seconds until melted. Add sugar, cracker crumbs and peanut butter; mix well. Spread into prepared pan.

MICROWAVE chocolate in microwaveable bowl on HIGH 1½ to 2 minutes or until melted, stirring after each minute. Cool slightly, then pour over peanut butter mixture in pan. Cool. Cut partially through dessert to mark 48 squares. Refrigerate 1 hour or until set. Lift from pan, using foil handles. Cut all the way through dessert into squares.

Makes 4 dozen or 24 servings, 2 squares each.

HOW TO MAKE THICKER SQUARES: Reduce chocolate to 1 package (8 squares). Prepare recipe as directed, using 9-inch square baking pan. Cut into 24 squares to serve.

Makes 2 dozen or 24 servings, 1 square each.

fast & fabulous entertaining

An assortment of party-perfect, stress-free desserts
sure to wow your guests

CHOCOLATE CLUSTER-PEANUT BUTTER CAKE

Total: 1 hour 20 minutes (includes cooling)

  1 package (2-layer size) chocolate cake mix

  1 cup cold milk

  1 package (4-serving size) **JELL-O** Vanilla Flavor Instant Pudding &
    Pie Filling

  ½ cup peanut butter

  ½ cup **PLANTERS** Dry Roasted Peanuts

  2 squares **BAKER'S** Semi-Sweet Baking Chocolate, melted

  1½ cups thawed **COOL WHIP** Whipped Topping

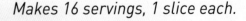

PREHEAT oven to 350°F. Prepare cake batter as directed on package; pour evenly into 2 greased and floured (9-inch) round cake pans.

BAKE 25 minutes or until toothpick inserted in centers comes out clean. Cool in pans 10 minutes; remove to wire racks. Cool completely. Meanwhile, pour milk into medium bowl. Add dry pudding mix. Beat 2 minutes or until well blended. Add peanut butter; beat well. Refrigerate until ready to use.

MIX peanuts and melted chocolate; stir until evenly coated. Drop by tablespoonfuls onto wax paper-covered baking sheet. Refrigerate 10 minutes or until firm.

PLACE 1 of the cake layers on cake platter; spread with 1 cup of the pudding mixture. Cover with remaining cake layer. Gently stir whipped topping into remaining pudding mixture. Spread over top and side of cake. Decorate with chocolate peanut clusters. Cut into 16 slices to serve. Store leftover cake in refrigerator.

Makes 16 servings, 1 slice each.

BLACK FOREST DELIGHT

Total: 4 hours (includes refrigerating)

1 package (2-layer size) devil's food cake mix

1¼ cups water, divided

1 package (4-serving size) **JELL-O** Cherry Flavor Gelatin

⅔ cup **BREAKSTONE'S** or **KNUDSEN** Sour Cream

⅔ cup powdered sugar

1 tub (8 ounces) **COOL WHIP** French Vanilla Whipped Topping, thawed

⅓ cup drained maraschino cherries, divided

1 square **BAKER'S** Semi-Sweet Baking Chocolate, melted

PREPARE and bake cake mix as directed on package in 2 (8- or 9-inch) round pans. Run knife or metal spatula around sides of pans to loosen cake layers. Cool 15 minutes.

BRING 1 cup of the water to boil; stir into dry gelatin mix until completely dissolved. Add remaining ¼ cup water. Pierce cake layers with large fork at ½-inch intervals. Carefully pour half of the gelatin mixture over each cake layer. Refrigerate at least 3 hours.

MIX sour cream and powdered sugar in medium bowl; gently stir in whipped topping. Dip 1 cake pan in warm water 10 seconds; invert onto serving plate. Spread cake with 1 cup of the whipped topping mixture. Reserve a few cherries for garnish. Chop remaining cherries; sprinkle over cake. Invert second cake layer onto wire rack; carefully place cake on first cake layer. Frost top and sides of cake with remaining whipped topping mixture. Drizzle with melted chocolate. Garnish with reserved cherries.

Makes 16 servings, 1 slice each.

> **TIP:** Substitute regular **COOL WHIP** Whipped Topping for French Vanilla Whipped Topping.

CHOCOLATE CREAM ORNAMENT CAKE

Total: 1 hour 20 minutes (includes cooling)

- 1 package (2-layer size) chocolate cake mix
- 1 package (4-serving size) **JELL-O** Chocolate Flavor Instant Pudding & Pie Filling
- 1 package (8 ounces) **PHILADELPHIA** Cream Cheese, softened
- 1 cup powdered sugar
- 1½ cups thawed **COOL WHIP** Whipped Topping
- 1 ice cream cone
- 1 piece red string licorice (2-inch)

  Decorations: colored sugar, small candies, additional red string licorice

PREHEAT oven to 350°F. Lightly grease 2 (9-inch) round cake pans. Prepare cake batter as directed on package. Blend in dry pudding mix. Pour evenly into prepared pans.

BAKE as directed on package. Cool 10 minutes; remove from pans to wire racks. Cool completely. Meanwhile, beat cream cheese and powdered sugar in small bowl with electric mixer on medium speed until well blended. Add in whipped topping; stir until well blended.

PLACE 1 of the cake layers on serving plate; spread with one-third of the cream cheese mixture. Cover with remaining cake layer. Spread top and side of cake with remaining cream cheese mixture. Poke 2 small holes in bottom of ice cream cone; insert ends of 2-inch licorice piece into holes, leaving small loop at top. Place cone next to cake to resemble ornament handle. Decorate top of cake with remaining ingredients as desired. Store in refrigerator.

Makes 16 servings, 1 slice each.

JELL-O Magic Mousse
"Layers Magically Separate During Refrigeration"

Total: 8 hours 10 minutes (includes refrigerating)

    3 cups boiling water
    1 package (8-serving size) **JELL-O** Cherry or Lime Flavor Gelatin
    1 tub (16 ounces) **COOL WHIP** Whipped Topping, thawed (**COOL WHIP**
       16-ounce tub mold can be found in the freezer aisle for a limited
       time only)

STIR boiling water into dry gelatin mix in medium bowl at least
2 minutes until completely dissolved. Add whipped topping to hot
gelatin; stir with wire whisk until whipped topping is completely
melted and mixture is well blended. (Mixture will still be thin.)

WASH whipped topping tub mold; dry well. Spray with cooking spray.
Fill with gelatin mixture.

REFRIGERATE 8 hours or overnight until firm. Unmold onto serving
plate just before serving. Store leftover dessert in refrigerator.

Makes 10 servings, about ½ cup each.

CHOCOLATE DRIZZLE GARNISH: Melt 1 square **BAKER'S** Semi-Sweet
Baking Chocolate in microwaveable bowl on HIGH 1 minute; stir
until melted. Cool slightly. Pour into resealable plastic bag. Snip
off small piece from one of the bottom corners of bag; squeeze
chocolate over serving plate as desired. Refrigerate until firm.
Unmold dessert onto prepared plate just before serving.

CHOCOLATE-COVERED CHERRIES: Pat maraschino cherries dry with
paper towels; set aside. Microwave 2 squares **BAKER'S** Semi-Sweet
Baking Chocolate in microwaveable bowl on HIGH 1 minute; stir
until melted. Dip cherries in chocolate; place on wax paper-covered
baking sheet. Refrigerate until firm.

HOW TO UNMOLD: Gently run knife around edge of mold and gelatin
to loosen. Dip mold in warm water about 15 seconds. Unmold onto
serving plate.

REYNOLDS FUN SHAPES:

Place 10 **REYNOLDS** Fun Shapes Baking Cups on 15×10×1-inch baking pan. Spray each cup lightly with cooking spray. Prepare recipe as directed; pour evenly into cups. Refrigerate 2 hours or until set. Unmold before serving. Drizzle with melted chocolate.

EASY ENGLISH TRIFLE

Total: 3 hours 30 minutes (includes refrigerating)

1 package (8 ounces) **PHILADELPHIA** Cream Cheese, softened

2 cups cold milk, divided

1 package (4-serving size) **JELL-O** Vanilla Flavor Instant Pudding & Pie Filling

1 package (10.75 ounces) pound cake, cut into 21 slices

1 package (10 ounces) frozen strawberries in syrup, thawed, drained and halved, syrup reserved

½ cup orange marmalade

2 cups thawed **COOL WHIP** Whipped Topping

BEAT cream cheese and ½ cup of the milk in large bowl with electric mixer on medium speed 1 minute or until well blended. Add dry pudding mix and remaining 1½ cups milk; beat on low speed 1 minute.

BRUSH both sides of pound cake slices with reserved strawberry syrup; set aside. Mix drained strawberries and marmalade. Place one-third of the cake slices on bottom of 2-quart clear glass serving bowl, cutting slices to fit. Layer with one-third each of the strawberry and pudding mixtures. Repeat layers 2 times. Cover surface with wax paper or plastic wrap.

REFRIGERATE several hours or until chilled. Top with whipped topping before serving. Store leftover dessert in refrigerator.

Makes 14 servings, about ⅔ cup each.

SUBSTITUTE: Substitute 50 **NILLA** Wafers for the pound cake.

fast & fabulous entertaining

WHITE CHOCOLATE LACE CUPS

Total: 15 minutes

  2 squares **BAKER'S** Premium White Baking Chocolate

  2 teaspoons grated orange peel

  ¼ cup thawed **COOL WHIP** Whipped Topping

  ¼ cup raspberries

LINE each of 2 medium muffin cups with a piece of **REYNOLDS** foil. Place in freezer 5 minutes. Meanwhile, microwave chocolate in small microwaveable bowl on MEDIUM (50%) 1½ minutes; stir until chocolate is completely melted.

DRIZZLE chocolate with a spoon onto bottoms and up sides of prepared muffin cups. Freeze 5 minutes. Carefully remove foil cups from pan; gently peel off and discard foil.

STIR orange peel into whipped topping; spoon evenly into chocolate cups. Top with the raspberries.

Makes 2 servings, 1 filled chocolate cup each.

> **MAKE AHEAD:** Unfilled chocolate cups can be stored in the freezer for up to 3 months. Remove from freezer and fill as directed just before serving.

FUDGE BOTTOM CHEESECAKE

Total: 1 hour 15 minutes

- 1 package (11.1 ounces) **JELL-O** No Bake Real Cheesecake
- 2 tablespoons sugar
- 5 tablespoons margarine, melted
- 1 tablespoon water
- 3 squares **BAKER'S** Semi-Sweet Baking Chocolate
- 1 tablespoon margarine
- 1½ cups cold milk
- 1 cup thawed **COOL WHIP** Whipped Topping

MIX Crust Mix, sugar, the 5 tablespoons melted margarine and the water with fork in 9-inch pie plate until well blended. Press firmly against side of pie plate first, using your finger or large spoon to shape the edge. Press remaining crumb mixture firmly onto bottom, using bottom of a dry measuring cup.

MICROWAVE chocolate and 1 tablespoon margarine in small microwaveable bowl on HIGH 1½ minutes or until margarine is melted. Stir until chocolate is completely melted; cool slightly.

BEAT milk and Filling Mix with electric mixer on low speed until well blended. Beat on medium speed 3 minutes. (Filling will be thick.) Stir 3 tablespoons of the filling into melted chocolate; spread evenly into crust. Top with remaining filling. Refrigerate at least 1 hour. Top each serving with 2 tablespoons of the whipped topping. Store leftover cheesecake in refrigerator.

Makes 8 servings, 1 slice each.

FUDGE BOTTOM CHEESECAKE TARTS: Press prepared crust mixture firmly onto bottoms of 12 paper-lined medium muffin cups, using spoon or bottom of glass. Prepare Filling mixture as directed. Spoon 1 heaping teaspoonful of the chocolate filling over each crust; top with the remaining filling. Refrigerate and store as directed. *Makes 12 servings.*

MOIST CARAMEL APPLE CAKE

Total: 1 hour 35 minutes

    1 package (2-layer size) yellow cake mix
    1 package (4-serving size) **JELL-O** Vanilla or French Vanilla Flavor
      Instant Pudding & Pie Filling
    1 cup water
    4 eggs
    ⅓ cup vegetable oil
    3 medium Granny Smith apples, peeled, coarsely chopped
   20 **KRAFT** Caramels, unwrapped
    3 tablespoons milk

PREHEAT oven to 350°F. Grease and flour 12-cup fluted tube pan or 10-inch tube pan. Beat cake mix, dry pudding mix, water, eggs and oil in large bowl with electric mixer on low speed until blended. Beat on high speed 2 minutes. Gently stir in apples. Pour into prepared pan.

BAKE 50 minutes to 1 hour or until toothpick inserted in center comes out clean. Cool 20 minutes; remove from pan. Cool completely on wire rack.

MICROWAVE caramels and milk in microwaveable bowl on HIGH 1½ minutes, stirring every 30 seconds until blended. Cool 10 minutes until slightly thickened. Drizzle over cake.

Makes 16 servings.

> **JAZZ IT UP:** Serve topped with thawed **COOL WHIP** Whipped Topping.

LUSCIOUS CREAM PUFFS

Total: 45 minutes

½ package (17.3 ounces) frozen puff pastry (1 sheet), thawed

1 cup milk

1 package (4-serving size) **JELL-O** Vanilla Flavor Instant Pudding & Pie Filling

½ cup thawed **COOL WHIP** Whipped Topping

1 square **BAKER'S** Semi-Sweet Baking Chocolate, melted

PREHEAT oven to 400°F. Unfold pastry sheet on lightly floured surface; roll pastry out to 10-inch square. Cut into 9 (3-inch) rounds using cookie cutter or rim of a glass. Place on ungreased baking sheet. Bake 10 minutes; cool completely.

MEANWHILE, pour milk into large bowl. Add dry pudding mix. Beat with wire whisk 2 minutes or until well blended. Gently stir in whipped topping. Cover. Refrigerate 15 minutes.

CUT cream puffs horizontally in half. Spoon pudding mixture evenly into bottom halves of cream puffs; cover with tops. Drizzle with melted chocolate. Serve immediately. Or, cover and refrigerate until ready to serve.

Makes 9 servings, 1 cream puff each.

SUBSTITUTE: Prepare as directed, using **JELL-O** White Chocolate Flavor Instant Pudding & Pie Filling and **COOL WHIP** French Vanilla Whipped Topping.

COFFEE-CARAMEL NUT TART

20 Minute Prep

Total: 1 hour 20 minutes

1¼ cups **HONEY MAID** Graham Cracker Crumbs

¼ cup (½ stick) butter or margarine, melted

3 tablespoons firmly packed brown sugar

¼ teaspoon ground cinnamon

35 **KRAFT** Caramels

⅓ cup whipping cream

1 tablespoon **MAXWELL HOUSE** Instant Coffee, any variety

3 cups **PLANTERS** Pecan Pieces, toasted

1 square **BAKER'S** Semi-Sweet Baking Chocolate, melted

PREHEAT oven to 325°F. Mix graham cracker crumbs, butter, sugar and cinnamon. Press firmly onto bottom and 1 inch up side of 9-inch springform pan. Bake 10 minutes or until lightly browned. Cool on wire rack.

PLACE caramels, cream and coffee granules in large microwaveable bowl. Microwave on HIGH 2 to 3 minutes or until caramels are completely melted, stirring after each minute. Stir in pecans; spread evenly over crust.

REFRIGERATE 1 hour or until firm. Drizzle chocolate evenly onto 12 dessert plates just before serving. Cut tart into 12 slices; place 1 slice on each plate. Store leftover tart in refrigerator.

Makes 12 servings, 1 slice each.

HOW TO MELT AND DRIZZLE CHOCOLATE: Place unwrapped chocolate square in microwaveable bowl. Microwave on HIGH 1 minute or until chocolate is almost melted; stir until chocolate is completely melted. Spoon into small plastic bag. Fold down top of bag; snip a tiny piece off 1 of the bottom corners of bag, about ⅛-inch wide. Holding top of bag tightly, drizzle chocolate back and forth onto dessert plates.

MAKE IT EASY: No time to make a scratch graham crust? Omit the graham crumbs, butter, brown sugar and cinnamon from recipe and use 1 **HONEY MAID** Graham Pie Crust (6 ounces) instead.

TRIPLE LAYER EGGNOG PIE

Total: 3 hours 15 minutes (includes refrigerating)

- 10 **KRAFT** Caramels
- 1 cup cold milk, divided
- 1 **HONEY MAID** Graham Pie Crust (6 ounces)
- ½ cup **PLANTERS** Chopped Pecans, toasted
- 1 cup cold eggnog
- 2 packages (4-serving size each) **JELL-O** Vanilla Flavor Instant Pudding & Pie Filling
- 1 tub (8 ounces) **COOL WHIP** Whipped Topping, thawed, divided

PLACE caramels and 1 tablespoon of the milk in microwaveable bowl. Microwave on MEDIUM (50%) 30 seconds or until caramels are completely melted when stirred. Pour into crust; sprinkle with pecans.

POUR remaining milk and eggnog into large bowl. Add dry pudding mixes. Beat with wire whisk 2 minutes or until well blended. (Mixture will be thick.) Spoon 1½ cups of the pudding over pecans in crust.

ADD half of the whipped topping to remaining pudding; stir until well blended. Spread over pudding layer in crust; top with remaining whipped topping. Refrigerate at least 3 hours before serving. Store leftover pie in refrigerator.

Makes 10 servings, 1 slice each.

JAZZ IT UP: Sprinkle pie with ground nutmeg or ground cinnamon just before serving.

CHOCOLATE-MINT PARFAIT

Total: 30 minutes (includes refrigerating)

2 cups cold milk

¼ teaspoon peppermint extract

1 package (4-serving size) **JELL-O** Chocolate Flavor Instant Pudding & Pie Filling

6 drops green food coloring

1 cup thawed **COOL WHIP** Whipped Topping

Additional **COOL WHIP** Whipped Topping (optional)

POUR milk and peppermint extract into medium bowl. Add dry pudding mix. Beat with wire whisk 2 minutes or until well blended; set aside.

ADD food coloring to the 1 cup whipped topping; stir gently until well blended. Layer pudding and whipped topping alternately in 6 parfait glasses.

REFRIGERATE at least 15 minutes before serving. Top with additional whipped topping, if desired.

Makes 6 servings, 1 parfait each.

SUBSTITUTE: Substitute ¼ teaspoon almond extract or ½ teaspoon ground cinnamon for the mint extract to customize the flavor of these parfaits.

delicious desserts for kids

Fun, simple recipes kids will love to make and devour

GINGERBREAD PEOPLE

Total: 1 hour 32 minutes (includes refrigerating)

¾ cup (1½ sticks) butter, softened
¾ cup firmly packed brown sugar
1 package (4-serving size) **JELL-O** Butterscotch Flavor Instant Pudding & Pie Filling
1 egg
2 cups flour
1 teaspoon baking soda
1 tablespoon ground ginger
1½ teaspoons ground cinnamon

BEAT butter, sugar, dry pudding mix and egg in large bowl with electric mixer on medium speed until well blended. Combine remaining ingredients. Gradually add to pudding mixture, beating well after each addition; cover. Refrigerate 1 hour or until dough is firm.

PREHEAT oven to 350°F. Roll out dough on lightly floured surface to ¼-inch thickness. Cut into gingerbread shapes with 4-inch cookie cutter. Place on greased baking sheets.

BAKE 10 to 12 minutes or until edges are lightly browned. Remove from baking sheets. Cool on wire racks. Decorate as desired.

Makes 20 servings, 1 cookie each.

MAKE IT EASY: To easily decorate these cookies, fill a resealable plastic bag with prepared frosting. Seal the bag and cut a small corner off the bottom of the bag. Roll down the top of the bag to squeeze the frosting over the cookies to decorate as desired.

delicious desserts for kids

HOLIDAY JELL-O JIGGLERS

10 Minute Prep

Total: 3 hours 10 minutes (includes refrigerating)

2½ cups boiling water (Do not add cold water.)

2 packages (8-serving size each) **JELL-O** Gelatin, any flavor

STIR boiling water into dry gelatin mix in large bowl at least 3 minutes until completely dissolved. Pour into 13×9-inch pan.

REFRIGERATE at least 3 hours or until firm.

DIP bottom of pan in warm water 15 seconds. Cut into 24 decorative shapes using 2-inch cookie cutters, being careful to cut all the way through gelatin to bottom of pan. Lift **JIGGLERS** from pan. Reserve scraps for snacking. Store in tightly covered container in refrigerator.

*Makes 2 dozen or 24 servings,
1 JIGGLERS each.*

MAKE IT EASY: Instead of cutting out with cookie cutters, cut the **JELL-O JIGGLERS** into 1-inch cubes.

delicious desserts for kids

HOT COCOA MARSHMALLOW CUPCAKES

Total: 1 hour 45 minutes (includes cooling)

- 1 package (2-layer size) devil's food cake mix
- 2 cups **JET-PUFFED** Miniature Marshmallows, divided
- 4 squares **BAKER'S** Semi-Sweet Baking Chocolate, coarsely chopped
- ¼ cup milk
- 1 tub (8 ounces) **COOL WHIP** Whipped Topping, thawed
- 1 tablespoon unsweetened cocoa

PREPARE and bake cake batter as directed on package for 24 cupcakes; cool completely.

MEANWHILE, place 1 cup of the marshmallows, the chocolate chunks and milk in large saucepan; cook on low heat until marshmallows and chocolate are completely melted and mixture is well blended, stirring constantly. Cool at least 30 minutes. Gently stir in whipped topping.

FROST cupcakes with the whipped topping mixture; top with the remaining 1 cup marshmallows. Sprinkle evenly with cocoa. Cover and refrigerate until ready to serve. Store leftover cupcakes in refrigerator.

Makes 24 servings, 1 cupcake each.

> **HELPFUL HINT:** Instead of making cupcakes, bake cake batter in 13×9-inch baking pan as directed on package. Continue as directed.

delicious desserts for kids

WIGGLIN' JIGGLIN' CUPCAKES

Total: 3 hours 45 minutes (includes refrigerating)

2½ cups boiling water (Do not add cold water.)

2 packages (8-serving size each) **JELL-O** Cherry Flavor Gelatin

1 package (2-layer size) yellow cake mix

1 tub (8 ounces) **COOL WHIP** Whipped Topping, thawed

Holiday sprinkles

STIR boiling water into dry gelatin mix in medium bowl at least 3 minutes until completely dissolved. Pour into 15×10×1-inch pan.

REFRIGERATE at least 3 hours or until firm. Meanwhile, prepare and bake cake mix as directed on package for 24 cupcakes. Cool completely on wire racks. Cut each cupcake in half horizontally.

DIP bottom of 15×10×1-inch pan in warm water about 15 seconds. Using 2-inch round cookie cutter, cut out 24 **JIGGLERS**. Place a small dollop of whipped topping on bottom half of each cupcake; top with **JIGGLERS** circle and another small dollop of whipped topping. Place top half of cupcake on each stack; press gently into whipped topping. Top with the remaining whipped topping and sprinkles.

Makes 2 dozen or 24 servings, 1 cupcake each.

JAZZ IT UP: Gently stir a few drops of food coloring into whipped topping before spreading on the cupcakes.

FAMILY FUN: Arrange prepared cupcakes in the shape of an ornament on a serving plate.

FESTIVE JELL-O POPCORN BALLS

Total: 1 hour 15 minutes (includes cooling)

¼ cup (½ stick) butter or margarine

1 package (10½ ounces) **JET-PUFFED** Miniature Marshmallows

1 package (4-serving size) **JELL-O** Gelatin, any flavor

3 quarts (12 cups) popped popcorn

Decorations: candies, sprinkles, string licorice and ribbon (optional)

MICROWAVE butter and marshmallows in large microwaveable bowl on HIGH 1½ to 2 minutes or until marshmallows are puffed. Stir in gelatin until well blended.

POUR marshmallow mixture over popcorn in large bowl; mix lightly until evenly coated.

SHAPE into 16 (2-inch) balls or other shapes with greased or moistened hands. Add decorations, if desired.

Makes 16 servings, 1 popcorn ball each.

> **JAZZ IT UP:** Wrap each popcorn ball in plastic wrap and tie with raffia or ribbon for gift-giving.

delicious desserts for kids

CHOCOLATE LOVER'S PIZZA

Total: 15 minutes

- 1 package (8 squares) **BAKER'S** Semi-Sweet Baking Chocolate
- 10 squares **BAKER'S** Premium White Baking Chocolate, divided
- 2 cups **JET-PUFFED** Miniature Marshmallows
- 1 cup crisp rice cereal
- 1 cup **PLANTERS COCKTAIL** Peanuts
- ¼ cup red maraschino cherries, well drained, halved
- ¼ cup green maraschino cherries, well drained, halved
- ⅓ cup **BAKER'S ANGEL FLAKE** Coconut
- 1 teaspoon vegetable oil

MICROWAVE semi-sweet chocolate and 8 squares of the white chocolate in 2-quart microwaveable bowl on HIGH 2 minutes; stir. Microwave an additional 1 to 2 minutes or until chocolates are melted, stirring every 30 seconds. Add marshmallows, cereal and peanuts; mix well.

SPREAD evenly into lightly greased 12-inch pizza pan. Sprinkle with cherries and coconut.

MICROWAVE remaining 2 squares white chocolate with oil in 1-cup microwaveable bowl on HIGH 1 minute; stir. Microwave an additional 30 seconds to 1 minute or until chocolate is completely melted, stirring every 15 seconds. Drizzle over coconut. Cool completely or refrigerate until firm. Store, covered, at room temperature.

Makes 20 servings, 1 wedge each.

> **INDIVIDUAL CHOCOLATE LOVER'S PIZZAS:** Divide chocolate mixture into 24 greased muffin cups; refrigerate until firm. Let kids create their own pizzas by adding their toppings of choice.

PEBBLES STOCKINGS

Total: 10 minutes

¼ cup (½ stick) butter or margarine

1 package (10½ ounces) **JET-PUFFED** Miniature Marshmallows

1 package (13 ounces) **POST** Fruity **PEBBLES** Cereal (about 8½ cups)

Decorations: decorating icings, chewy fruit snack rolls, sugar alphabet letters and assorted candies

MICROWAVE butter in 4-quart microwaveable bowl on HIGH 45 seconds or until melted. Add marshmallows; toss to coat. Microwave 1½ minutes or until marshmallows are completely melted and mixture
is well blended, stirring after 45 seconds. Stir in cereal.

SHAPE into 24 stocking shapes with moistened or greased hands, using about ⅓ cup of the cereal mixture for each stocking. Place on wax paper-covered tray. Cool. Add decorations as desired.

Makes 2 dozen or 24 servings, 1 stocking each.

SUBSTITUTE: Prepare as directed, using **POST** Cocoa **PEBBLES** Cereal.

The FLINTSTONES and all related characters and elements are trademarks of ©Hanna-Barbera.

holiday classics

Timeless classics and new dessert creations—a spectacular finale to any holiday feast

believe in holiday magic

CHOCOLATE-CANDY CANE CAKE

Total: 1 hour 40 minutes (includes cooling)

- 1 package (2-layer size) chocolate cake mix
- 1 package (4-serving size) **JELL-O** Chocolate Flavor Instant Pudding & Pie Filling
- 4 eggs
- 1 container (8 ounces) **BREAKSTONE'S** or **KNUDSEN** Sour Cream
- ½ cup vegetable oil
- ½ cup water
- 4 squares **BAKER'S** Semi-Sweet Baking Chocolate, chopped
- 18 small candy canes, coarsely crushed (about 1 cup), divided
- 1 tub (8 ounces) **COOL WHIP** Whipped Topping, thawed

PREHEAT oven to 350°F. Lightly grease 2 (9-inch) round cake pans. Beat cake mix, dry pudding mix, eggs, sour cream, oil and water in large bowl with electric mixer on low speed just until moistened, stopping frequently to scrape side of bowl. Beat on medium speed 2 minutes or until well blended. Stir in chopped chocolate and 2 tablespoons of the crushed candy canes. Spoon evenly into prepared pans.

BAKE 35 to 40 minutes or until toothpick inserted in centers comes out clean. Cool 10 minutes. Loosen cakes from sides of pans with metal spatula or knife. Invert cakes onto wire racks; carefully remove pans. Cool completely.

PLACE 1 of the cake layers on serving plate; spread evenly with 1 cup of the whipped topping. Top with remaining cake layer. Frost top and side of cake with remaining whipped topping. Sprinkle with remaining crushed candy canes just before serving. Store leftover cake in refrigerator.

Makes 18 servings, 1 slice each.

SUBSTITUTE: Melt 1 additional square **BAKER'S** Semi-Sweet Baking Chocolate; cool. Drizzle over cake just before serving. Then, garnish with raspberries.

FANTASY FUDGE

Total: 4 hours 25 minutes (includes refrigerating)

  3 cups sugar

  ¾ cup (1½ sticks) butter or margarine

  1 small can (5 ounces) evaporated milk (about ⅔ cup)

1½ packages (12 squares) **BAKER'S** Semi-Sweet Baking Chocolate, chopped

  1 jar (7 ounces) **JET-PUFFED** Marshmallow Creme

  1 cup chopped **PLANTERS** Walnuts

  1 teaspoon vanilla

LINE 9-inch square pan with foil, with ends of foil extending over sides of pan; set aside. Place sugar, butter and evaporated milk in large heavy saucepan. Bring to full rolling boil on medium heat, stirring constantly. Boil 4 minutes or until candy thermometer reaches 234°F, stirring constantly to prevent scorching. Remove from heat.

ADD chocolate and marshmallow creme; stir until completely melted. Add walnuts and vanilla; mix well.

POUR immediately into prepared pan; spread to form even layer in pan. Let stand at room temperature 4 hours or until completely cooled; cut into 1-inch squares. Store in tightly covered container at room temperature.

Makes 3 pounds or 40 servings, about 2 squares each.

> **USE YOUR MICROWAVE:** To prepare the fudge in the microwave, place butter in 4-quart microwaveable bowl. Microwave on HIGH 1 minute or until melted. Add sugar and milk; mix well. Microwave 5 minutes or until mixture begins to boil, stirring after 3 minutes. Stir well, scraping down side of bowl. Microwave 5½ minutes, stirring after 3 minutes. Let stand 2 minutes. Add chocolate and marshmallow creme; continue as directed.

FESTIVE CRANBERRY-PINEAPPLE SALAD

Total: 5 hours 40 minutes (includes refrigerating)

1 can (20 ounces) **DOLE** Crushed Pineapple, undrained

2 packages (4-serving size each) or 1 package (8-serving size)
JELL-O Raspberry Flavor Gelatin

1 can (16 ounces) whole berry cranberry sauce

1 medium **DOLE** Apple, chopped

⅔ cup chopped **PLANTERS** Walnuts

Apple Slices (optional)

DRAIN pineapple, reserving liquid in 1-quart liquid measuring cup.
Add enough cold water to reserved liquid to measure 3 cups; pour into
large saucepan. Bring to boil; remove from heat. Add gelatin; stir at
least 2 minutes until completely dissolved. Add cranberry sauce; stir
until well blended. (Note: Due to the presence of whole berries in the
cranberry sauce, the gelatin mixture will not be smooth.) Pour into
large bowl. Refrigerate 1½ hours or until slightly thickened
(consistency of unbeaten egg whites).

STIR in remaining pineapple, apple and walnuts; stir gently until well
blended. Pour into medium serving bowl.

REFRIGERATE 4 hours or until firm. Garnish with apple slices just before
serving, if desired. Store leftover gelatin in refrigerator.

Makes 14 servings, ½ cup each.

MOLDED CRANBERRY-PINEAPPLE SALAD: To serve as a molded
salad, substitute a 6-cup mold for the serving bowl. Also, use
1 can (8¼ ounces) **DOLE** Crushed Pineapple, ⅓ cup chopped
PLANTERS Walnuts and add enough cold water to the reserved
pineapple liquid to measure 2 cups.

Makes 10 servings, ½ cup each.

DOLE is a trademark of Dole Food Company, Inc.

DOUBLE LAYER PUMPKIN PIE

Total: 4 hours 20 minutes (includes refrigerating)

4 ounces (½ of 8-ounce package) **PHILADELPHIA** Cream Cheese, softened

1 tablespoon milk

1 tablespoon sugar

1 tub (8 ounces) **COOL WHIP** Whipped Topping, thawed, divided

1 **HONEY MAID** Graham Pie Crust (6 ounces)

1 cup milk

1 can (15 ounces) pumpkin

2 packages (4-serving size each) **JELL-O** Vanilla Flavor Instant Pudding & Pie Filling

1 teaspoon ground cinnamon

½ teaspoon ground ginger

¼ teaspoon ground cloves

MIX cream cheese, 1 tablespoon milk and the sugar in large bowl with wire whisk until well blended. Gently stir in half of the whipped topping. Spread into bottom of crust.

POUR 1 cup milk into large bowl. Add pumpkin, dry pudding mixes and spices. Beat with wire whisk 2 minutes or until well blended. (Mixture will be thick.) Spread over cream cheese layer.

REFRIGERATE 4 hours or until set. Top with remaining whipped topping just before serving. Store leftover pie in refrigerator.

Makes 10 servings, 1 slice each.

DOUBLE LAYER PECAN PUMPKIN PIE: Prepare as directed, stirring in ¼ cup chopped toasted **PLANTERS** Pecans along with the whipped topping.

HOLIDAY MIX & MATCH PUDDING PIE

Take 2 cups cold milk, 2 packages (4-serving size each) or 1 package (8-serving size) **JELL-O** Chocolate or Vanilla Flavor Instant Pudding & Pie Filling and 1 tub (8 ounces) thawed **COOL WHIP** Whipped Topping and mix & match your recipe from these options...

Recipe options	crust and filling choices	special extra possibilities
Peppermint-Chocolate	**HONEY MAID** Graham Pie Crust; 1 cup **JET-PUFFED** Miniature Marshmallows	10 peppermint candies, coarsely chopped; wedges of Peppermint Bark
Raspberry-Double Chocolate	**OREO** Pie Crust; 1 cup fresh raspberries	20 fresh raspberries; White Chocolate Curls; 2 teaspoons powdered sugar
Black Forest	**OREO** Pie Crust; 10 **OREO** Chocolate Sandwich Cookies, quartered	1 cup cherry pie filling; drizzle with 1 square melted **BAKER'S** Semi-Sweet Baking Chocolate
Banana-Caramel Chocolate	**OREO** Pie Crust; 1 cup sliced bananas	13 Chocolate-Dipped Pecans; 5 **KRAFT** Caramels melted with 1 teaspoon milk

Then follow our simple steps:

1. **POUR** milk into medium bowl. Add dry pudding mixes. Beat with wire whisk 2 minutes or until well blended. (Mixture will be thick.)

2. **SPOON** 1½ cups of the pudding into 1 (16-ounce) crust; top with filling. Gently stir 1½ cups of the whipped topping into remaining pudding; spoon over pie.

3. **REFRIGERATE** 3 hours. Cover with remaining 1½ cups whipped topping just before serving. Top with special extras. Store leftover pie in refrigerator.

Makes 10 servings, 1 slice each.

PEPPERMINT-CHOCOLATE PUDDING PIE

PEPPERMINT BARK: Microwave 4 squares **BAKER'S** Semi-Sweet Baking Chocolate in microwaveable bowl on HIGH 1½ to 2 minutes or until melted, stirring every 30 seconds. Stir in ¼ cup crushed peppermint candies (about 10 candies). Spread thinly onto wax paper-lined baking sheet; refrigerate until firm. Break into pieces; place on top of pie.

WHITE CHOCOLATE CURLS: Microwave 1 square **BAKER'S** Premium White Baking Chocolate on HIGH 15 seconds. Slowly pull a vegetable peeler along one side of the chocolate square to create a curl. Use wooden pick to arrange curls in center of pie.

CHOCOLATE-DIPPED PECANS: Microwave 1 square **BAKER'S** Semi-Sweet Baking Chocolate in microwaveable bowl on HIGH 30 seconds or until melted; stir. Dip one end of each pecan half in chocolate. Place on wax paper-lined baking sheet; refrigerate until firm. Arrange over pie.

WATERGATE SALAD

Total: 1 hour 15 minutes (includes refrigerating)

1 package (4-serving size) **JELL-O** Pistachio Flavor Instant Pudding & Pie Filling

1 can (20 ounces) **DOLE** Crushed Pineapple, in juice, undrained

1 cup **JET-PUFFED** Miniature Marshmallows

½ cup chopped **PLANTERS** Pecans

1½ cups (½ of 8-ounce tub) thawed **COOL WHIP** Whipped Topping

MIX dry pudding mix, pineapple, marshmallows and pecans in large bowl until well blended.

ADD whipped topping; stir gently until well blended. Cover.

REFRIGERATE 1 hour or until ready to serve.

Makes 8 servings, about ½ cup each.

JAZZ IT UP: Serve this treat in small individual dessert dishes garnished with a maraschino cherry.

DOLE is a trademark of Dole Food Company, Inc.

HOLIDAY POKE CAKE

Total: 4 hours 15 minutes (includes refrigerating)

- 2 baked (9-inch) round white cake layers, cooled
- 2 cups boiling water
- 1 package (4-serving size) **JELL-O** Gelatin, any red flavor
- 1 package (4-serving size) **JELL-O** Lime Flavor Gelatin
- 1 tub (8 ounces) **COOL WHIP** Whipped Topping, thawed

PLACE cake layers, top sides up, in 2 clean (9-inch) round cake pans. Pierce layers with large fork at ½-inch intervals.

STIR 1 cup of the boiling water into each flavor of dry gelatin mix in separate bowls at least 2 minutes until completely dissolved. Carefully pour red gelatin over 1 cake layer and lime gelatin over second cake layer. Refrigerate 3 hours.

DIP 1 cake pan in warm water 10 seconds; unmold onto serving plate. Spread with about 1 cup of the whipped topping. Unmold second cake layer; carefully place on first cake layer. Frost top and side of cake with remaining whipped topping.

REFRIGERATE at least 1 hour or until ready to serve. Decorate with fresh raspberries, if desired. Store leftover cake in refrigerator.

Makes 16 servings, 1 slice each.

SPECIAL EXTRA: For an easy, festive touch, sprinkle top of cake with holiday colored sprinkles just before serving.

index